FOREWORD BY JACQUELINE JAKES

BECOMING ENGAGED™
Finding the Courage to Be Me!

CHERYL L. THOMAS

Copyright © 2007 Cheryl L. Thomas

All Rights Reserved. No part of this book may be reproduced in any form or by any electronic or mechanical means, including information storage and retrieval systems, without permission in writing from the publisher, except by a reviewer, who may quote brief passages in a review.

Scripture quotations are taken from the Holy Bible, King James Version (KJV). Public domain.

Library of Congress Control Number: 2007905023
ISBN 978-0-9797717-0-5

Cover photo by *Mike Taylor*
Cover & Book Design by *M&N Marketing Group*

Published by:
BE Books
A Division of Becoming Engaged Enterprises, LLC
P.O. Box 382764
Duncanville, Texas 75138

DEDICATION

This book is dedicated to my parents, Mr. and Mrs. James and Annie Thomas. Thank you for your loving support and for never giving up on me. The person I am today is because God graced you to not only birth me, but also nurture, support and cultivate the gifts I had on the inside. I am forever grateful to you and deeply indebted to God for the gift of true parents. I love you forever!!

ACKNOWLEDGEMENTS

Nothing ever happens in a vacuum. There is always an army of individuals who God sends to help birth purpose and destiny in you. To my army: Sandy, Val and Lesley — my best friends in all the world. I thank God that He not only chose you as my sisters, but honored me with your friendship. I love you much. Joel, thanks for taking good care of Sandy and my girls. Now I finally have a brother. Yeah! To Nikki (for the great Myspace page designs) & Karlyne (for the impromptu book edits) — thank you for believing in your Auntie. Your words of encouragement lifted me when I was exhausted. You're both my favorite (smile).

Cameshia Davis — my accountability partner — I don't know how I would have done it without you. Thanks for allowing God to use you to speak words of encouragement to me. Your faith in the gift of God in me caused me to keep going when I was tired and ready to quit. I so appreciate your friendship. Ms. Daneca Norris — that prophetic gift is being stirred up in you. Keep moving forward and know you deserve God's best.

To Jacqueline Jakes — thank you for pouring *Sister Wit* into me before the world received it. Your wisdom is second to none and I know God placed you in my life for such a time as this. To Bishop & First Lady Jakes — over the past 10 years I've been living, breathing, talking and walking out the tremendous ministry God speaks through you both. I count it an honor and privilege that God allows me to call you my pastors.

Ann Fields — editor extraordinaire — I appreciate your diligence to the framework of this book. To my *Becoming Engaged*™ Club friends — the best is yet to come. To everyone else that had a hand in helping this book become a reality — words cannot express the gratitude in my heart. But God will repay.

TABLE OF CONTENTS

Foreword vii
Preface ix
Introduction xi

SECTION 1 WAKE UP
Chapter 1   Becoming Engaged 17
Chapter 2   The Courage to Be Me. 21
Chapter 3   Authentically Me 25
Chapter 4   Mirror Image. 29

SECTION 2 SHAKE UP
Chapter 5   Discovering Me. 35
Chapter 6   Fearfully and Wonderfully Made 39
Chapter 7   Captivated by the Light. 45
Chapter 8   Treasure Hunt 51
Chapter 9   Finding Contentment in Him 59
Chapter 10 Blind Faith 63

SECTION 3 LOOK UP
Chapter 11 The Journey to You 71
Chapter 12 Living in the Moment 77
Chapter 13 The Beauty of Now 81
Chapter 14 Be Alive 85

FOREWORD

I am often asked to speak at various functions around the country. Invariably, somewhere in the message I speak about a lady who has impeccable character and who has been a blessing to me for nearly a decade. I always mention her friendliness, faithfulness, her cheerful spirit and her loyalty to Christ and His Kingdom. Cheryl Thomas is that lady.

It is rare to stumble upon someone as genuine, consistent and perpetually a joy to be around. It's hard to hide your real personality when you work with people 8 hours a day, five to six days a week. It becomes nearly impossible to fake a good working relationship for that length of time. Cheryl is real. Really nice. Really well-raised. Really genuine and really fun. I cannot say enough good about this woman who has served, worked with me, stood by me and supported me in anything I've needed.

God has gifted her with an enviable character and personality. Her qualities, like all rare and precious gifts, have been paid with a price. However, she has taken her struggles and through her own personal development, harnessed and subdued her inconsistencies and her perplexities, until they bowed their knees to the treasure within her. She turned her straw into gold.

For nearly the past ten years she has served as a staff member of *The Potter's House* as my assistant and project coordinator for our *Partner Relations Department*. She is a model for today's young women and a treasure and pleasure to the aging and aged.

Once you engage to her thoughts and her presence, you'll be more refreshed, enlivened, informed and encouraged.

In her own words, let her tell you how Christ causes her to triumph and to shine.

—Jacqueline Jakes
jacquelinejakes.com

PREFACE

There's a great push to discover one's purpose and calling. Everybody's trying to figure out the formula. Trying to find out where they belong... where they fit. We're running from one conference this week to another conference/seminar the next week looking for answers no person can give. We ask our friends and family, "Who am I and why am I here?" We look for it in the latest, greatest movie star — maybe they can provide the perfect model or at least some of the answers to this dilemma. I, too, was on this rollercoaster ride. After years of searching, none of those resources held the answer my soul so desperately craved. Finally, I turned to the Creator of all things — the One I should have sought first for the answer.

What I learned from God, I scripted in the following pages. May you, through reading my desperate search find a shortcut for your journey. Yes, it is a journey. While traversing this long and treacherous path — it is sometimes seemingly never ending and unfair, but in the end or at the gracious middle — you'll discover something incredible. The road you travel leads right back to.... you.

INTRODUCTION

All of my life I was a great cheerleader. Gifted with the ability to encourage and champion others, I could point out so many wonderful qualities in others, yet I often found it difficult to encourage myself. I thought everyone else had his or her act together and it was me who had so much to learn, so much knowledge to gain, so much wisdom to obtain. I could never possibly hope to know what came to everyone else so easily. Surely they knew more, surely they were more qualified. I felt I would never be on their level. I felt they had some special gift that I didn't or never would have. I was so busy seeing what was wonderful in others that I never took the time to unearth God's wonder in me. According to His Word, I was wonder — *ful*; full of pleasure, excitement and incredible in His eyesight. It was amazing for a little country girl like me to realize God esteemed me wonderful. Believe me, it took me a long time to go from hearing that to receiving it.

Sometimes when you read God's thoughts about you in His Word it is hard to grasp that He is referring to you. We've been so inundated with everyone else's estimation of us that it is sometimes difficult to accept God's view of us.

But if His Word declares that I am the apple of His eye, would it be arrogant of me to say, "I am wonderful?" Would you think it bold to hear me say, "I'm simply incredible?" It may seem out of line to many Christians because we're often taught that kind of attitude is nothing short of prideful. But God's Word declares we are fearfully and wonderfully made. We're not afterthoughts, we're not what God created in a moment of boredom. We were carefully thought out and created with much anticipated, thoughtful care. We are God's elect, His chosen vessels. That alone makes us special. There is no other person on the face of the planet like you. There is something unique, special and all together lovely about the handiwork of the Lord in you.

Once we realize how special we are to God; how He watches diligently over us; how not a second goes by that we are not on His mind; and that it is His utmost desire to see us prosper, our own sense of esteem sharply rises. Now, I'm not talking about self-esteem. Self-esteem can fluctuate. One day you may feel good about yourself and the next — at the word or hushed whispers of others — you do not. What I speak of is what I call God-esteem: to know that the Lord of the Universe places unlimited value in us and our lives is mind-boggling.

When we understand that we are special to God, our sense of worth rises. We know that if God esteems us, then we can esteem ourselves. If He calls us beautiful, then it's the pure unadulterated truth because He is a God who cannot lie and His Word will not return unto Him void. We then must choose to accept God's thoughts even over our own. We must acknowledge His preeminence as the Creator and agree with His estimation because He has the last word over us. That takes trust. To lay aside everything everyone else has said and to even refute negative images of ourselves means we have to trust God's Word.

That is what it boils down to for most Christians — we don't trust. Or at least let me be honest about myself. I learned that I didn't truly trust Him. I wasn't leaning on Him. Somewhere along the road, I started carrying my burdens and problems. Now, it's arrogant to think that we are more equipped than God to handle our problems, but one of the hardest lessons for me to learn was to trust. I've been a born-again Christian since the age of 12, and at 30+ years, I'm just learning to trust God.

Since my born-again experience, I can say that I've been working — working to live a life that's pleasing to Him, working to live Holy, working to be a "good" Christian. But there was not a lot of trusting going on. Through a series of events, however, God showed me that though I claimed Him as Lord and Savior, though I'd surrendered my heart to Him, I hadn't surrendered my life. I guess I thought I should handle that. Surely God had enough to deal with without adding my life's issues. But I found I'd robbed both myself and God. I'd robbed myself of the peace and privilege of resting in

His ability and great desire to care for me. I'd robbed myself by enduring countless nights of worry and frustration. But most importantly, I'd robbed myself of the intimacy of His warm embrace and comforting words assuring me of His divine provision and protection. I'd robbed myself and God of deep fellowship.

What I had with God was not deep fellowship. It was the rote obedience of a fearful child — a child afraid that she wouldn't be loved if she did something wrong; a child that marked obedience with blessing. I did what I thought was right because I thought if I were good, God would bless and love me and if I wasn't, I felt His love would withdraw from me. I didn't realize that no matter my state — good, bad or ugly — He loved me nonetheless. His love for me was unconditional. He loved me because I was His.

Who can find a love like that? There is none. There will never be a person who can love completely and unconditionally. Man may come close, but there is no earthly love that fills all the empty places like God's love. His love can take a broken heart and mend it, take a wayward soul and reclaim it, but most importantly, it took a scared little girl and brought peace, healing and wholeness. I thank God for His amazing love!

In the pages that follow, allow me to take you on the journey that produced within me the ability and the courage to be exactly who God created me to be. You'll find *Ringmasters*, which are Scriptures to reinforce concepts introduced within the book, *Rules of Engagement*, which offer reflections and food for thought and finally *Engagement Rings*, which offer exercises to help you take your dreams and make them reality. Welcome to the greatest adventure ever — your life!

Section 1

WAKE UP

"Life is happening all around you."

Chapter 1

BECOMING ENGAGED

The Awakening

> **Rule of Engagement**
>
> Before you can muster the courage to be yourself, you have to understand who you really are. Beneath all of the titles, all of the assumptions, and setting aside other people's opinions — do YOU know? You can't reject anyone's perception if you haven't defined or decided who you are. Without God it is impossible to do. Take off all of the masks and uncover God's wonder in you.

On my first cruise to the Caribbean, I sat on the rear of this amazing vessel and looked out over the sea to the approaching island. I stared in awe across the crystal azure waters glistening in the sunrise. As I raised my hand to my now moist face, I suddenly realized I had been crying for some time. I cried at the beauty I had never before witnessed. I cried because I was afraid my family would never see it. I also cried because this spectacular seascape had been there all along and I was just getting the opportunity to enjoy it. It filled me with wonder.

I wondered what other beauty God had hidden all over the earth that I had not availed myself? What other hidden jewels had He tucked away for me to discover? That simple tropical sunrise was a defining moment for me. God revealed to me that I wasn't taking advantage of my passage through the viaduct of time. He brought the Scripture John 10:10 to my attention and told me I was not living. He came, suffered, died and rose again so that I could live! I had received His salvation, but hadn't learned how to access His life. I decided in that moment that I wasn't going to continue to exist this way anymore. So began my journey to live the God-life; the glorious, overcoming, productive life that He specifically ordained for each of us.

As I began to explore this new brand of living, I realized that in order to really live this kind of life you had to know who you were on the inside. Did I know who I was in the pit of my soul, my being? The answer was an unfortunate no. I'd become so accustomed to living life on my terms and the terms of those around me that I really couldn't say that I knew how God saw me nor who He created me to be. I knew that if I was going to live an abundant life — one that would be so attractive that it would draw others to Him — I would have to pour my whole self into learning God's plan and purpose for my existence and then begin to voraciously live the life Jesus planned for me.

This experience taught me what makes me happy, what energizes and keeps me and what makes me feel rested, relaxed and renewed. Learning these and other things about myself made my life richer and I couldn't wait to translate my experiences and inspire others to find their path to the God-kind of life. God gave up His most precious gift — His Son — to offer us life. We, as Christians, owe it to Him to take advantage of this gift and live so well that the world will want to know who we are, whose we are and seek to know the God we serve.

We must not fear life, but embrace it, nurture it and develop our capacity to not only receive it, but to give it. Christ gave us life so that we in turn could minister life to others, but unless we know what life is we are in no position to give the life He came to give. We must now take up our mantle to fulfill the mission Christ died to impart — the ability to give life. We, as Christians, must teach the world to live. And to truly live you must live the God-kind of life!

Rule of Engagement

When people see you, they should see a picture of your Heavenly Father. Live your life so well and so richly that it pleases your Father and brings the world to His feet.

Chapter 2

THE COURAGE TO BE ME

> **Ringmaster**
>
> *Have not I commanded thee? Be strong and of a good courage; be not afraid, neither be thou dismayed: for the LORD thy God is with thee whithersoever thou goest. Joshua 1:9*

I don't know if there are others like me out there, but for most of my life I tried to live up to everybody's expectations. I admit it. I was an addict, a people pleaser. I was addicted to the praise of others. Now, praise works fine until you inevitably do something wrong. It is only a matter of time before you do something that someone, somewhere, for some reason dislikes. What happens then? You begin the rollercoaster ride of high and low self-esteem. A ride I didn't get off until my late 30's. After 30+ years of living at the mercy of other people's opinions, I finally decided I'd had enough. I was going to be myself, do what I wanted and live how I wanted whether it pleased others or not. I was tired of trying to live up to unspoken expectations.

Yes, you heard me right — unspoken expectations. You see it was not that I was bowing to demands from others. No, that would have made my exodus much easier. Unfortunately, I was bowing to the expectations I perceived others to have of me. No one ever vocalized any ridiculous or otherwise expectation. Most of my fear and trauma came from my assumptions. I assumed that if my friendships and relationships were to grow and flourish then I would need to be the perfect friend — available at all times, to do anything. That was just my warped way of thinking. Surely no one would want to be with me just for me. Could it be true that I was just good company — nice and a pleasure to be around? I never gave myself that much credit. This attitude flowed into almost every area of my life. But one day I just decided I was tired. Tired of pretending it was okay that I was always there for people who were hardly ever there for me. I was tired of being taken advantage of and taken for granted. I was tired of going above and beyond for everyone else and leaving myself out.

After giving my best to everyone else, often I had very little strength left for myself. I decided to do something radical. I gave myself permission to be good to me — FIRST! I'd always been good to myself and pampered myself when I could, but it was generally AFTER taking care of everybody else. I came to the realization that I was important too and if no one else took the time to celebrate me, then I would celebrate myself.

> **Engagement Ring**
>
> *Do you consider yourself a priority? Select a day this week to treat yourself. Whether the treat is a cup of your favorite coffee, a quiet walk in the park or a few moments alone, make sure to include yourself on your list of "special" people!*

COURAGEOUS LIVING!

What is courage? Is it bravery? Or is it the lack of fear? I've come to believe courage isn't the lack of fear, but it is the steel nature to stare one's fear in the face. There have been a myriad of obstacles or fears that I've had to face: the fear of rejection, the fear of success, the fear of failure, but most notably the fear of being myself. I know that may sound ridiculous, but it is nonetheless true.

What do you do when you fear people won't like you, or that your feelings, thoughts or opinions will be rejected? What some of us do is hide. We only show the side of ourselves that we believe others will approve. Hiding is a lot of work and it is such an awful, terrible place of fear. You're cut off from the world, cut off from reason and cut off from reality. This is a dangerous place to be because it leaves you open to the deception, lies and trickery of the enemy. When you're all alone, you have no one to combat those lies so the enemy constantly bombards you with subtle deceit and paranoia. You begin to look at everyone with warped, unbalanced focus.

Hiding was and still is one of the hardest challenges I've ever faced, but after hiding for over three decades, I was exhausted. Thank God for maturity. I believe age brings with it a liberty and freedom like nothing else does. Suddenly, the opinions of others cease to matter as much as your own. You begin to become comfortable in your own skin and therefore more comfortable releasing and exposing your vulnerabilities. Hiding is no longer an option. You are finally ready to be REAL.

Ringmaster

According as he hath chosen us in him before the foundation of the world, that we should be holy and without blame before him in love. Ephesians 1:4

Chapter 3

AUTHENTICALLY ME

> **Ringmaster**
>
> I have chosen the way of truth: thy judgments have I laid before me. Psalm 119:30

Fake. Phony. Those are words that we often use to describe others we feel are not showing their "true" selves. These people are typically viewed critically and are people whose presence we may tolerate but do not enjoy. There is nothing more painful than to spend precious time, moments you can never retrieve, with someone who is fake. However, if we examine our lives closely, I'm sure there are moments when we ourselves have worn a few masks.

The church world is especially riddled with this phenomenon. It is a world that can perpetuate hypocrisy. I know that hypocrisy is a strong word, but as a person who has spent her entire life in the church,

I know all too well there is this unspoken feeling that if you're truly a Christian, things must always be perfect. You must have the perfect mate, perfect children, a perfect career, house, car, investment account and retirement plan.

But what would "they" say if they knew you weren't perfect? What would they think if it became public knowledge that you had a few struggles and were God-forbid, human? I believe the Body of Christ needs a reality pill — one that allows us the privilege of being people. We serve God, we are NOT HIM. We all have faults, flaws and shortcomings. No one is perfect. Now everyone may not embrace your delicate combination of imperfections, but then again they don't have to. You are a distinct individual and not everyone is called to join you in your journey in life.

Rule of Engagement

What side of yourself could you be hiding from the world? What rich treasure is the world not privy to because of your fears? Take the opportunity today to bless your world with a glimpse of the beauty God placed within you!

It took me some time, but I came to a point where I began to truly accept the fact that everyone was not going to like me or enjoy my company. It was liberating! I also faced the fact that there were going to be people whose company I didn't prefer nor enjoy. And that was okay. I finally gave myself permission to be an individual — not a group, nor part of a set. I was uniquely crafted and created, designed by the Creator of the universe. He placed within me certain likes, dislikes and dispositions. I wasn't serving the world by attempting to conform to their likes or pleasures. I was actually robbing them of the wonderful and unique gift God made when He birthed me. I decided that if people were going to dislike me, which some inevitably would, they were going to dislike the real me. Not someone I was pretending to be to gain favor. If there were going to be darts and missiles thrown my way, it would be because they saw the exquisite creation of God and rejected it. If I am rejected for this, then that is okay.

I have learned to be myself — not who I think people want me to be, not the picture perfect image I would like to portray to others, but simply and honestly myself. I used to be afraid to let others see the "not-so-pretty" side of me. I thought that if every hair was not in place, if I didn't say all the right things, if someone saw me angry or upset or if my attitude was a wee bit sour, people would reject me.

I've since learned to let those close to me know all sides of me. What that has allowed me to know is that there are people who love me just as I am — warts and all. It's what I call being authentically me. There is no one in the entire universe quite like me. No one looks like me, behaves like me, or has the exact personality I have. When someone encounters me, they have had a one of a kind experience. They will not ever repeat that experience at any time during their life on this earth.

And if by chance they have the opportunity to meet or greet me again, that experience will be totally new and unique because I'm ever evolving and growing in my relationship with Christ.

    I have spent years moving towards the completed picture He sees when He looks at me and I do believe with all of my heart that I take a step closer to my purpose and destiny everyday.

Chapter 4

MIRROR IMAGE

> **Ringmaster**
> *But we all, with open face beholding as in a glass the glory of the Lord, are changed into the same image from glory to glory, even as by the Spirit of the Lord. 2 Corinthians 3:18*

Have you ever looked in the mirror for a long time? I mean a really long time — the time it takes for reflection; reflection on who you see before you. As a young girl I was fascinated with my reflection in the mirror. I would stand in front of the mirror for hours talking to myself. I've always had an extremely vivid imagination. I could sit for hours and plot stories; I would be in my own little world. To this day I can still do it. Storylines and plots live within my mind. I guess it's one of the reasons I'm a writer. Or maybe I write because God placed these stories within me.

As I now look in the mirror, sometimes I become somewhat frightened. Not because of the reflected image, but because of what I "see" that's not visible to the eye. Have you ever looked at yourself and sensed that you were peering past your flesh and deep into your very own soul? When you look past your exterior, what or whom do you really see? I mean, past the make-up, the fancy clothes, the career, the husband/wife and children — who are you? Really? How would you describe yourself?

Could you form one sentence that would let a stranger know the essence of your personality without it being attached to someone or something else? What is your greatest desire, achievement and longing? What feeds your soul and enriches your spirit? How do you spell relief? How do you recharge? Do you recharge? What makes life worth living for you? Who are you pouring into and why? What keeps you going/motivated? What/who do you turn to when your well has run dry or when you feel overwhelmed? Are you at the top or bottom of your list of priorities? Are you even on the list? Are you too busy being busy?

Are you really accomplishing anything or just spinning your wheels? How do you define success? How much money or stuff is enough and who decides that for you? Is your quest for man's definition of success quietly chipping away at the very fiber of your soul? Have you ceased to be your true self, but rather a cheap version of the expectations of those around you? These are a lot of questions, but ones that I believe every person must answer on their journey.

If you don't answer these questions for yourself, then you allow the world to tell you who you are. That means others are creating a life for you and you are not living a true authentic life. Don't take the passenger seat in your own life and allow others to dictate who you should be, where you should live, who you should marry, what the best career is for you and what or what not to pursue.

I believe we do ourselves an incredible disservice when we do our best to know others, but have not made the same effort to know ourselves. Getting to know yourself is a lifelong task, but it is one that you must tackle to live a life that is fulfilling.

You must take time to learn who God created you to be. Decide that you will lay aside everyone's definition and roadmap for you and decide to plot your own life. Live your own dreams and make sure the dream you pursue is truly yours. You must ask yourself, this dream I chase, is it my desire or is it the dream of another? Perhaps it is a dream you thought others would admire, but you have neither the desire nor passion to pursue it. If you're going to expend the incredible energy it takes to chase your dreams, they must be yours. You are serving no one, especially not yourself, to chase a dream that is not God-ordained nor God-inspired. It may be a great dream and aspiration for someone else, but if it is not a part of your purpose, drop the counterfeit dream and trust God to reveal His dream for you.

Engagement Ring

To really "know" yourself, you have to dig deep. You have to look beyond the mere surface and the superficial things most people notice. Transfix on your own reflection in the mirror and ask yourself who you are. Set aside what other people say or have said. This is not about the opinions of others. This is your survey. What is unique about you? Is it your sense of humor, your unique style, your giving spirit or infectious zest for love and life? What do you have to offer the world that no other person can? This is a divine appointment to be self-absorbed. Educate yourself about who you are.

Section 2

SHAKE UP

"You are unique and divine — embrace it. Throw off all inhibitions and begin to love the 'real' you!"

Chapter 5

DISCOVERING ME

> **Ringmaster**
>
> *A gift is as a precious stone in the eyes of him that hath it: whithersoever it turneth, it prospereth. Proverbs 17:8*

I absolutely love singing and music. Just hearing a melodic verse has the ability to change my mood and lift my spirit. As a child I could envision my glowing music career. I knew my CDs would race up the charts as I shared my singing gift with the world. In my shower and in my personal devotion time, I was Gospel's greatest undiscovered talent. I was great in my own mind. Now don't get me wrong, I am a "mean" background vocalist, but God did not gift me with the necessary skill to sing lead powerfully. I had to take inventory of my true talents and be honest with myself.

Though I wasn't able to sing like Aretha, God did give me an awesome gift to write. So although the world would not rock to the sound of my voice, if I was diligent, maybe they could hum the lyrics God would anoint me to write. Through trial and error and honest evaluation, I was beginning to zero in on my true gifting.

God would not place a dream within you to be a famous recording artist and not also equip you with the talent to sing beautifully and with power. If no one validates your gift of song, you may want to rethink or revisit this dream. It could be a dream born out of the flesh, the desire to please or the desire for fame and fortune. On your journey to discovering you, you've got to be really honest with yourself.

Make sure you're not pursuing vain imaginations. This is like chasing the wind; it is a waste of time and an underutilization of your true skills and birthright as a born-again Christian. Do not spin your wheels seeking fame only to obtain it and find you're still not fulfilled. Run in the direction of God's dream for you. This simply means chasing or exploring the path of your gifts. If you zero in on the areas that excite and motivate you and seek ways to explore or create opportunities centered on your gifts and talents, you'll find yourself closing in on your God-ordained purpose.

When you first begin seeking God for purpose, you may feel overwhelmed. There may be so many dreams locked in the pit of your soul, you find it hard to figure out which dream to pursue first. You must pray for divine direction. Now, I wish I could tell you that in several weeks or months you will have the answer, but several years passed before I even caught a glimpse of an answer surfacing. You heard right — a glimpse of an answer.

What I've learned from my searching and seeking is that sometimes God unfolds your purpose in layers. He doesn't always reveal everything at once. In His timing, when He knows you're ready, He unveils a piece of the puzzle. Today, I'm still unraveling and unfolding layers of His purpose for my life. It keeps me on my face constantly seeking His wisdom and direction.

Never lose sight of your goal. Yes, it will take time, but the outcome is sure because God will complete the work He began in you.

> **Rule of Engagement**
>
> *What gifting could you be overlooking in yourself? We are sometimes so enamored with the gifts and talents of others, we fail to unearth the enormous treasure within ourselves. Dig in your own treasure chest and release your God-given gifts.*

Chapter 6

FEARFULLY AND WONDERFULLY MADE

> ### Ringmaster
> I will praise thee; for I am fearfully and wonderfully made: marvellous are thy works; and that my soul knoweth right well.
> Psalm 139:14

The closer I get to God and the more I know and understand Him, the more I know myself. I am learning that we cannot truly know ourselves without knowing Him. Therefore, the journey to fully knowing who we are must begin with the journey to know and love our God. We are, after all, created in His image and likeness. We are a product of the original and we have our Father's genes. Everything He is, we are. Everything He has, so do we. We are His workmanship.

This means we were neither a rush job nor an afterthought. He was mindful as He created us. He knew exactly what we would need on our journey. He knew the personality we'd need. The disposition we'd need. He knew the level of intellect our life would require and took all of this and more into account when He created us.

But He didn't stop at creation. As He planned our lives, He made sure we would encounter the right people, endure the right trials, witness the right situations and enter the right family. He began at the end, taking into account every situation we would need to build Godly character so that our lives would be a representation of His handiwork.

Every day, every moment and every second of our life has been mapped out and divinely planned. We are simply walking in footprints that He already paved and carved out to guide us along the way. No more is this realized than when we reach an area or time in our life that seems perfect; like we've "come home." Have you ever had that experience? That you were at the right place at the right time with the right people? You feel as though all is right with the world. It is then that you know you've stepped into the very footprint of God who came and made the way before you.

It is our daily endeavor to go this route, the one He divinely set for us, and the one that has His seal of approval. We may come up short sometimes, but we strive daily to keep our eyes and ears attuned to the next set of instructions that will lead us closer to Him and therefore that much closer to ourselves.

> **Rule of Engagement**
>
> You are God's treasure. Never give in to the enemy's lie. Know that you are accepted in the beloved.

A Class of One

Our world doesn't typically celebrate individuality. Ours is an environment that promotes the lie of "normal." Everyone is expected to march to the beat of the same drummer and simply fall in line with the popular train of thought. Anyone who deviates from that avenue is either ostracized, ignored or abandoned.

I've always known I was different. Even as a child, there was seemingly no place where I truly fit in. For a young child that can be devastating. So you can imagine what a misfit I felt like growing up. I was a huge baby, but a small petite child. Okay, I'll admit it; I was quite the scrawny little thing. Like many smaller kids, I was picked on mercilessly.

Today I am still small framed — a size two to be exact. My physical stature fools many people. Most people never realize my age because of my size. Although this serves me well now, that was not always the case. I can distinctly remember being with my friends and being addressed as their daughter. What was funny to everyone else irritated, frustrated and angered me because I was so eager to grow up.

I never knew God would use my size and youthful appearance as a vehicle to draw young people to Him. But from my youth up to now He has strategically used me to speak into the lives of young people. Whether it was a young girl facing an identity crisis or a young man seeking counsel on his place in the world, young people would seek my advice on a myriad of topics. I didn't understand it then, but I came to realize that they saw me as one of them. They could relate to me and therefore trusted me in ways they never trusted adults of my same age. My appearance also serves as what I call "the greatest advertisement for early salvation." Saved at the tender age of 12, I sometimes comically comment to others that God is using my appearance to show the world how He preserves His own.

  In addition to being small, I was also a gifted student and typically the only one or one of a few African Americans in a classroom environment, which also contributed to my being the constant brunt of everyone's jokes. From one thing to the next, I always seemed to be singled out. I didn't understand it then, but God was teaching me how to walk alone. He was training me in the art of aloneness.

  It has taken me a long time to accept my inherent difference, but I've finally rested in my unique style and presence and accepted it as God's gift to me. It is incredible to know there has never been, nor will there ever be anyone like me. I am in a class all by myself. Which begs the question, why? What do I have to offer the world that no one else can? What gifts and talents do I impart that cannot be harvested in anyone else? What is my unique contribution to the world? I came to know and realize, if I am here, there is something within me I am to use to bless the world.

Every one of us has a unique gift to offer the world. When God's Word says we are fearfully and wonderfully made, we must know our very presence on this earth means we have something that no other human has. For some that talent may be the gift to encourage. For others, it may be a sweet, soothing presence or it may be the bubbly contagious joy that lifts our hearts when life's trials have battered our soul. Whatever your unique treasure, do not hide it. The world is in dire need of it.

Engagement Ring

What sets you apart? What do you do easily that others struggle to do? What do you love? What brings you "pure" joy? As you answer these questions, look deep within yourself to see the treasure God has placed within you.

Chapter 7

CAPTIVATED BY THE LIGHT

> **Ringmaster**
>
> *Let your light so shine before men, that they may see your good works, and glorify your Father which is in heaven. Matthew 5:16*

Have you ever felt like there was a special gifting in you that God was going to use to bless others? I know it may sound arrogant, but I believe God hides the light of greatness in us all. God places a gift in His children and our countenance illuminates because of it. It can be equated to a woman who is pregnant. It is not only her physical appearance that helps us recognize she is carrying a child. When you see her, she appears to beam. It is as if her entire being lets you know she is carrying precious cargo.

When you carry God's gifting within you, your whole person emits light because you have God within you.

I vaguely remember the first time I recognized God's gifting within me. I can't tell you how I knew it was God. There was no audible voice or earth-shattering event that caused me to recognize Him. But I knew it was God. I must admit, it scared me. I couldn't believe the God of the universe was deciding to use me. Did He know who I was? Surely He'd made a mistake. In my mind, there were people who were more talented, more courageous and more charismatic. Here I was, this little country Florida girl and He'd put this enormous treasure within me.

As I was growing up, every now and then God would give me a sneak peek or quick flashes of this gift He had hidden in me. Sometimes it was a prophecy concerning my life that confirmed what I already felt in my spirit. Other times it was a dream that clearly showed my future. Having this gift frightened me. So I did the only thing I knew to do. I hid it and tried to wish it away. I placed the light of His gift under a bushel. Or so I thought. But even without my saying anything, people could still see the light. I could be silent and enter a room and feel as if I was being watched. It didn't just happen in church circles. It happened everywhere. In the grocery store, at the gas station, in restaurants. The light was inescapable. It drew so much attention from others that it made me take notice. Thus my journey to the light started. What was I supposed to do? I was lost and longing. The curiosity became desire, desire became need. I had to know why He had apprehended me. It became as important to me as inhaling my next breath.

Rule of Engagement

Where is God shining His light in your life? Investigate your past and find clues to your story.

As I started my search, the light was dim. I knew I was gifted with several talents; I just wasn't sure how they were to work in tandem to accomplish my purpose in life. I thought if I could just figure out the direction of my purpose, I would know how to align my gifts to accomplish it. The light began to brighten as God revealed that my purpose would not bring me to my gifts, but that my gifts would unveil the direction of my purpose.

It was then that I began to chase my gifts. I sharpened the skills I knew I had and developed those that others saw in me. As I continued to explore and cultivate my gifts, I got closer to destiny and purpose. The more I sharpened my gifts, the brighter the light became and the less I feared exposure to it. This revelation also shed light on my fears.

I realized my fear of the light rested on a few factors. One of which was the fear of success. I know that might sound strange, but I feared success a lot more than I did failure. My fear of success was because I didn't want to stand under the expectations of people. I also didn't know if I was ready for the responsibility of success. Success is great, but it brings with it immeasurable weight, expectations and responsibilities. Many have fallen under the pressure of the light, many have grown arrogant under the deception of false light and many have been burned by success because they failed to realize that the light was God's and not their own. I didn't want nor did I think I was prepared for the stress of the light God placed within me. It has taken me quite a while to not fear and hide the light. There are times when I still retreat, but I'm learning everyday to embrace and cultivate it so I can begin to reproduce it.

> **Rule of Engagement**
>
> *Are you shrinking or hiding from God's light within you? What makes you retreat? Call on the courage of the Lord to help you stand firm as you uncover His plan for your life.*

Racing Toward the Light

The thing that finally caused me to cease my retreat was surprising. It was still fear, but a fear far greater than the fear of success and exposure to critics. It was the fear of displeasing my heavenly Father and the fear of regret.

I knew the great investment God had in me. I decided I couldn't live knowing I'd taken that investment for granted and turned away at the sound of His call. It hurt my heart to realize I was saying no to the gift He had so graciously imparted within me simply because I was afraid — afraid of public opinion; afraid that I would disappoint Him or that I would not be received. I decided that pleasing Him meant more to me than the possible jeers and rejection from others. I simply could not refuse Him. He'd paid too much, given too much. No matter how great my fear, I would not allow it to stop me. I would push forward beyond the fear until I was smack dab in the center of His will.

The other fear was regret. I did not want to look back over my life and ask the question, "What if?" Yes, I was afraid to move forward, but I was more afraid to not be able to look back at my life and say I'd done all I could or all I'd been asked to do. Today these two fears still keep me moving forward when satan tries to stop my progress.

As the light became brighter and my calling clearer, I finally began to rest in Him. I accepted the fact that I did not choose this path; He chose it for me. And since He chose me, He would guide me in the path, purpose and destiny He selected for me. All I had to do was follow His lead and listen closely for His voice.

But to do that, I had to learn His voice. How was I supposed to learn His voice? I had no one to teach me how to hear God. I asked others how they knew when God was speaking to them. I wanted some kind of barometer or better yet, a lesson plan on how to hear from God. What I learned was that God speaks in a multiplicity of ways.

I have three sisters and we all share the same father. He loves us all greatly, however, I noticed that he does not talk to each of us in the same way. Even though we are very close in age, we have very different personalities. The eldest, Sandy, is the nurturing mother hen. Second is Valerie, a tell-it-like-it-is woman. Third is Lesley, ever the diplomat; and last is myself, a little bit of it all. My father knows this and addresses each of us accordingly. So it is with God. As our Creator, He knows exactly what to say and how to say it to achieve the desired results from us.

When I finally stopped questioning how everyone else heard from Him, I began to look back over my life to see how God communicated with me. I realized that often I heard the voice of God through life's circumstances. God made pivotal moves in my life when He was ready to take me in another direction. Hearing His voice came in the form of His closing doors, so I had no other choice but to move on. God would speak to me this way because He knows me. He knows that I am loyal to a fault. He knows that once I am comfortable and complacent in any situation, He must often render that place barren before I'll finally take the hint and move on. As I mature, I am getting better at detecting His voice, but there are times when I still need a gentle nudge. His nudges often come in the form of His revealing a little more light on my future and my purpose. He knows I sometimes need motivation to move forward. A simple glimpse of purpose feeds my spirit and provides the encouragement I need to press on.

As you continue to seek God, rest assured that at the moment you're most distressed, He will send someone or some way to reveal to you a peek of your future. No matter how dim your light may seem know that it is the gift of God waiting to manifest within you. Be encouraged and keep racing toward His light.

Chapter 8

TREASURE HUNT

> **Ringmaster**
>
> But we have this treasure in earthen vessels, that the excellency of the power may be of God, and not of us. 2 Corinthians 4:7

Society has a way of locking you in. Or maybe the reality is that we lock ourselves in with our own thinking. Do you sometimes allow yourself to be limited by other people's expectations of you? Do you sometimes even hinder your progress because you don't see the potential God has placed on the inside of you? If we could fathom the depths of our gifting, if we could tap into the power God has placed on the inside of us, it would blow our minds. In the Word it says, "We have this treasure hidden in earthen vessels." I'm sure most of you are aware of this Scripture. The question then becomes, do you believe it applies to you? Do you believe God has placed His treasure in you? When you are convinced of this, your journey intensifies.

The journey to discover and unearth this treasure is sometimes a long, arduous one. It is full of winding roads, dark alleys, back roads and seemingly dark forests. You'll encounter detour signs along the way that lengthen your journey. There will also be a few yield signs. These are some of the hardest signs to obey, as they allow others to journey ahead of you and birth patience in you.

You'll see a few merge signs as God brings or aligns ordained partnerships where there is mutually beneficial enjoyment. There will also be diverging roads that will tear you away from unhealthy, toxic relationships. These roads are especially bumpy because often we do not know what is good for us and sometimes God has to snatch us out of situations we've become comfortable with and would not leave on our own. He'll extract us from partnerships in which we are embedded and find hard to escape without His loving help. This is all a part of the treasure hunt. It is all a part of what I call excavating the soul.

When you commit to exposing God's gift inside of you, know it is not all pain. It is also an immensely rewarding journey full of joy. You will leap for joy to find you are His treasure, His workmanship and the apple of His eye. And when He begins to reveal the jewels inside of you, your heart will rejoice to know that He trusts you with such priceless commodities. Gifts of encouragement, healing and administration are signs of the favor and trust He has in you. To realize the Lord of the universe trusts us to this degree is mind-boggling.

God gives gifts to us, not that we might boast on the greatness of our gift, nor the level of trust He has in us, but that we might take those gifts and multiply them. He is a wise investor and is looking for a return on His investment. Every day provides us with the opportunity to do something, anything, to further enhance, cultivate and encourage the growth and maturity of that gift.

> **Rule of Engagement**
>
> *When Jesus returns, what will you have to show in response to His great investment in you? Have you utilized your gifting to its fullest potential? Is your gifting lying dormant or have you buried it in fear? At His return there will be no room for excuses. You will have to give an account for your effort or the lack thereof. Decide today to use every moment to uncover God's treasure in you.*

Great Impressions

I remember sitting in a room with my classmates as we listened to my elementary school teacher describe all the things we could do and be when we grew up. Our little minds swam thinking of all the possibilities. We could be doctors, lawyers, politicians, or even actors and actresses. As she described all these wonderful professions, my mind buzzed with heady expectations of all I could accomplish.

She then went around the room to ask each student the famous question, "What do you want to be when you grow up?" At the tender age of seven or eight, each student told their career aspirations. The room would fill with oohs and ahhs as the list became more and more impressive. Now, I am a natural show person who "kinda" likes the spotlight. So even as a child, I sat thinking what career I could say to attract or draw the most applause.

An overachiever as a child, I was used to being called smart, was in accelerated and gifted courses most of my life and found school easy. I liked being "impressive." So if I thought something I did would cause celebration or praise, that's what I would do.

Most of my life was spent that way. A lot of the opportunities I chased were for the applause and accolades of men. I was addicted to praise. It took me a long time to admit to myself that living a life that was impressive to others was draining me. I wasn't happy. I wasn't fulfilled. I was cheating my soul of its uniqueness.

When I stopped living to please others, I began the journey to please myself. I decided to do the things I thought I would enjoy only to find I really didn't know myself well enough to even discern what I liked. I had to learn what made me happy; what made me sad; what relaxed me; what energized me.

The major thing this self-evaluation did for me was to bring me to the feet of Jesus. I knew I couldn't have a true understanding of who I was without constant conversation with the ONE who created me. So the questions I asked were directed more to God than to myself. As I asked these questions, I looked to God for the answers. It was a great time of reflection for me as I had to quiet the noise in my soul long enough to hear my Savior speak volumes to me about myself.

> **Engagement Ring**
>
> What really matters is not who you are to yourself or even who you want to be. The real emphasis should be on who God created you to be. Are you becoming what He had in mind when He thought of you? Do you reflect that now? If not, what are the steps you need to take to make sure that happens?

Sweet Surrender

It was amazing to hear God tell me who I was in Him. He would take me through different periods in my life that I had totally erased from my memory to reveal strengths and gifts He'd sharpened in me through life's trials. I remember specific times when He would remind me of ways He'd used me to speak life into someone's situation where I had no frame of reference. I listened as He explained that He'd gifted me with the word of knowledge and the gift of wisdom. It was in these moments that He showed me who He created me to be. I may have had my plans and designs on who I would be when I grew up, but when I grew up in Him, He showed me His plans.

While He was revealing His treasure within me, He was showing me glimpses of where He was taking me. Sometimes the picture was too great for me. Often I couldn't imagine what He saw in me. With this insight, there was only one thing to do... surrender. That has been the simplest, yet hardest task for me to learn. Surrender. How do you do this? How do you, after years of struggle, settle and quiet yourself long enough to accomplish this task?

I had to pray and consecrate myself as I began to release and surrender my plans so I could accept His. This has not been an easy task. But there is one truth that keeps looming in the back of my mind that helps me let go. It is the realization that if in all of the years that I chased my dreams, I didn't find fulfillment, just maybe following God's plans would bring me real joy.

I remember when I accepted my call to minister. It was such a scary thing. I'd been in the presence of people who ached to be in ministry; people who saw it as a glamorous life. I couldn't believe they actually wanted to minister. I wanted to do anything but minister. Somehow, I knew at an early age the sacrifice necessary to fulfill this call and I wasn't sure that I had the goods, or if I wanted to be bothered. I loved my freedom and the ability to plot and plan my life without the scrutiny of others.

I also understood the gravity and weight of the call. It is no small thing to carry God's message and be entrusted with the care of His precious souls. To think that people look to you to hear from God is scary. Especially when you're human and sometimes struggle to hear from Him yourself. I thought, "Lord, this is too high for me. Please give this mantle to someone more equipped." I just wanted Him to rethink His choice of me. Better yet, I wanted Him to choose someone else.

After initially accepting my call into ministry, I thought I could bargain with God. I decided that I didn't have to necessarily preach; I could be a motivational speaker. That way, I could use my gift of encouragement and my gifting to teach and still be in line with God's plan for me. I learned that you cannot bargain with God to restructure your destiny. While motivational speaking may be another avenue in which God chooses to use me, I know my main focus is ministry.

God's gift in me was His treasure and I was treating it like trash because I didn't feel worthy nor did I want the responsibility. Sometimes we are afraid of the vastness of the treasure within us because we can clearly see our flaws. We are so busy inspecting our imperfections that we fail to spend time refining the treasure. As you reflect on your own life remember to polish the treasure within you and give the frailty of your vessel to Jesus.

Rule of Engagement

Does your dream and God's plan collide? Are you struggling to accept God's plan for your life? Understand that His plans are always the best, even when we don't understand. Decide today to surrender your plans and accept His because only then will you find peace and contentment.

Chapter 9

FINDING CONTENTMENT IN HIM

> **Ringmaster**
>
> *Thou wilt shew me the path of life: in thy presence is fulness of joy; at thy right hand there are pleasures for evermore. Psalm 16:11*

Everyone who has found their life's goal or purpose talks about how fulfilling their life is. When I see the gleam in the eyes of people who are walking in their purpose, it makes my soul ache to find and walk in my purpose. However, what these warriors forget or fail to mention is how lonely and sometimes treacherous the road to destiny. They didn't tell me that the closer I got to unveiling God's purpose for my life, the more people He would peel away from my circle of friends.

They didn't mention the heartbreak I would go through with broken friendships, betrayal and envy. I wasn't aware that the closer I got to God, dear friends and amiable associates would give me the cold shoulder, make snide remarks and be disrespectful. I was the same person who they once seemed to love, however, now it seemed as if I was being shunned. I was totally caught off guard and hurt by the mistreatment. But the lessons I learned on my lonely road to finding purpose and destiny were priceless.

I learned how to trust God in a way that I hadn't up until that point. I learned the fragility of human relationships. I learned that people are fickle. One day they will sing your praises and the next day they will despise you for no reason. I learned the only safe place for my trust was Jesus. I thank God for those times of testing because it settled me in a way that has anchored me solely to the foundation of His Word.

Ringmaster

Trust in the LORD with all thine heart; and lean not unto thine own understanding. Proverbs 3:5

Stripping away certain people was God's way of getting me alone. He knew the work that He needed to perform required me to depend solely on Him. So He stripped me of all my crutches. Every other place that I would have leaned on, He took away. Every resource dried up. I had to call on Him. It was in this place of solitary confinement that I learned who God was; hence I learned who I was. These were the most precious moments during which I received God not only as my Creator, but also as my loving Father. It was in those moments of duress and despair that He held me close.

There's nothing or no one who can soothe your soul like Jesus. I know this because after life shattered every piece of my heart, I looked up towards my heavenly Father and said, "Lord, I don't know how you are going to fix this. My heart is torn into so many tiny pieces; I can't even find them all. So if you could, please find them, gather them and mend my broken heart." It was then that He took every single piece of my heart and with more love than words can express, gathered them all and with the skill of a master surgeon massaged my heart back to perfect health.

Rule of Engagement

Life has a way of chipping away at your courage. Whether it is a hurtful event from your past or your own inhibitions, you must decide to move forward.

Chapter 10

BLIND FAITH

> **Ringmaster**
>
> *For I know the thoughts that I think toward you, saith the LORD, thoughts of peace, and not of evil, to give you an expected end.*
> *Jeremiah 29:11*

God's plans for us are always bigger and greater than our plans for ourselves. Here I was making huge plans for my life to impress other people, while the Master's plans for me were so much greater. When God showed me glimpses of my destiny, it filled me with awe and wonder. I didn't see how I could fit into the magnificent plans He had for me. How would I ever measure up? Could I really do this?

It is sometimes daunting to see yourself operating inside of the plans God has for you. He sees so much in us. Things we never see in ourselves. He believes in the gifts/talents He placed in us, not because we are great, but because He is great. He knows His gifts are powerful and if directed and used appropriately, they will yield maximum results.

After I surrendered my plans for my life and embraced God's plans, I was still somewhat fearful. What if it didn't work? What if I didn't measure up? What if I failed God? What if after I proclaimed to the world God's incredible plan for me, I realized I'd heard incorrectly? Following God has truly been a walk of faith. I have had to step out and walk on the Word I believe God spoke over my life.

Desiring to walk out God's plan and actually executing it are two separate things. There were many times when I heard an incredible sermon that added to my faith in God's plan for me, but the moment I decided to actually put works to that faith the whispers of the enemy would ring out. I had to learn how to disregard the voices and opinions of others and walk toward the vision I believed God had shown me.

It's been rather challenging. There have been many times when I've had to chase doubt and fear away along with insecurities and self-consciousness. I had to trust that the God who had begun a good work in me would complete it. I knew this was not a journey I'd begun on my own. It was a divine mission. I've often heard people say, 'If you didn't start it, you're not obligated to finish it.' So my prayer has been, "Lord, you started this ministry in me and I'm looking for you to complete it. I'll do whatever you say and go wherever you say go. As long as I know you're with me, all is well."

> ## Engagement Ring
>
> *Are you courageously following God's path? What fear is keeping you stuck? List three fears that may be hindering your progress. Face one fear head-on this week and move into God's glorious plan for your future.*

I was born to carry His Word. Every gift, every tool, every talent that I need to accomplish and fulfill my purpose, God has buried within me. However, being built for your purpose doesn't mean it will come without a price. As I stated before, it is not going to be without struggle, heartaches and many tears. There will be sacrifices you must make and it is often a very lonely road. But the passion He births in you for your calling will be so great, you will withstand the pressure to accomplish His purpose.

Not everyone who begins the journey will complete it, for it takes great courage and blind dedication to follow God. Sometimes He gives you a roadmap. Other times — more often than not in my experience — it is truly a faith walk.

Rule of Engagement

Whose measuring stick are you using in life? Is it your own or that of your family and friends? Decide that only God has the measure of your worth. If He declares you worthy, then everyone else's opinion ceases to matter.

Jesus: The True Measure

It's always so inspiring to hear others talk of their walk of faith. When they describe how God took them from poverty to prosperity, sickness to health and discouragement to joy, it does wonders for our faith. However, when the trial hits you those testimonies seem to fade in the distance because while these faith giants were declaring to us their great victory in detail, it seems they somehow skipped or skimmed over the horrid details of the trial.

Sometimes in an effort to encourage others we fail to tell the unadulterated truth. Maybe we're afraid to be totally transparent for fear of judgment. We may wonder, "What would people really think if they knew how often I've felt like giving up?" "How would people react to know I would sometimes just like to quit?" We wonder if people would think we were great if it were known that we sometimes struggle with fear. Would others seek our advice or direction if they knew every step we took was by faith?

We often feel we must have it all together all of the time. But what if we don't? Is there anyone who can be trusted with our shortcomings? Can we show vulnerability to anyone who won't uncover or breach confidence? This is real pressure, the pressure to perform, to be perfect and to deliver.

Pride has often caused us to allow others to place us on pedestals that only Christ deserves. It's a dangerous place to be. We are human — we are not God! We can never allow anyone, or ourselves, to elevate us beyond the place of servant. People are insatiable. They will require of and from you things no human should ever be asked to perform. We cannot be Christ for them. We can only point them to Him. When we occupy our place as messengers correctly, I believe a lot of the stress and pressure will be alleviated. We won't try to live up to the world's expectations, but live our lives to fulfill God's expectations. He said His yoke was easy and His burden light. To serve at optimum capacity, we must take off the burdensome yoke of the expectations of people and only accept the yoke of Christ. He is the only One to whom we must answer.

We must decide to live using God's measure and estimation of us because that is all that really matters.

Ringmaster

Being confident of this very thing, that he which hath begun a good work in you will perform it until the day of Jesus Christ.
Philippians 1:6

Section 3

LOOK UP

"God's opinion of me is the ONLY one that matters. I agree with who He has called me to be."

Chapter 11

THE JOURNEY TO YOU

> **Ringmaster**
>
> *The eyes of your understanding being enlightened; that ye may know what is the hope of his calling, and what the riches of the glory of his inheritance in the saints. Ephesians 1:18*

Have you ever looked at an object so long that everything else around it became blurry? That's what it means to focus. To put everything else that is not directly related to your goal, dream or pursuit out of your mind and fix your gaze on the object of your intent/desire. Focus is what it takes when you're attempting to learn who you are in Christ and who He has destined you to be.

To begin the journey of focus, you must learn who

God calls you. You must scour the Scriptures to have His Word ingrained in your spirit so when the enemy comes with false identity, you can look him in the face and say, "No devil, that is not who I am. I do not accept that." You must rehearse the Word and say, "I am fearfully and wonderfully made. I am His workmanship and was chosen in Him before the foundation of the world. I am the apple of His eye." This is something you must KNOW. It can't just be something you hear or read. You have to know that if He cared enough to create you, watch over your life and carry you through life's tests and trials safely that He has a love for you that defies description.

He loves you so much that He sent His only Son as a sign of His incredible love and commitment. He was so focused on redeeming us that nothing deterred Him from reclaiming us. That's the kind of focus we need to unearth our true identity in Christ. An unrelenting, tenacious focus that says, "I will not stop until I discover why He apprehended me." He could have chosen anyone, but He sought you out, He chased you, and knocked at the door of your heart until He captured you. Even when you rejected His pursuit, He kept on coming. Even when you gave up, He never did. Even when you decided it wasn't worth the struggle, He said you were worth the trouble. A love that focuses like that is unstoppable.

> ## Rule of Engagement
>
> *Focused – a fixed, planted gaze. Is your gaze firmly planted on your future or do you find yourself allowing situations to distract you? To secure your destiny you will have to sharpen your focus. You cannot allow anything or anyone to deter you from reaching your goal.*

When you decide knowing your purpose and destiny is tantamount to your existence, your focus sharpens. You become relentless and will not let go until He renames you. Like Jacob at Peniel, you strive with Him, waiting for Him to tell you who you are. It doesn't matter how long it takes — weeks, months or years — you keep searching for that answer like water for a thirsty soul. And when it comes — when God names you — it removes all fear and intimidation of men. It no longer matters what other people say about you.

When the God of the universe declares you are righteous, holy, set apart and beloved, all is right with the world and so you go forth on the journey to you. You cease to live at the shrine of other people's opinion of who you are or should be. You now only listen out for one voice — God's. It is His voice you long to hear, encouraging you when you're tired and discouraged; enlightening you when you're confused; directing you when you've somehow lost your way. His voice becomes life to you.

You seek it early in the morning and late at night. Better than any companion, sweeter than anything is the voice of the Lord to a searching soul.

> ## Rule of Engagement
>
> *Do you feel God's unconditional love for you? Do you know what it feels like to be loved unconditionally? Imagine how you would feel knowing someone loved you in spite of all your faults and shortcomings. That is exactly what Christ's crucifixion displayed - His incredible/ unconditional love for you. Embrace it.*

At the beginning of 2006, I selected the first three months as a season of consecration for myself. I would fast once a week and on that day I would steal away to pray and seek God's will and direction for my life. I was purposing to align myself with God's perfect will. I felt this was a pivotal year — a defining season — in my life. For that reason I knew I had to quiet my soul to better hear and know His plans for me. The time I'd set apart with Jesus was an awesome time of sharing, reflection, meditation and renewal. I learned more about myself in those three months than I had in several years. Like a flower opening its bud for the first time, God was revealing who He created me to be.

During this time He affirmed how much He cares for and adores little old me. To be adored by God is mind-boggling. To know that He is mindful of me feeds my soul. Though everyone else around me disappears, His constant abiding presence grounds and centers me. To have the undivided attention of your Creator and to know without a doubt that His love for you is pure and without motive or fine print conditions is awesome. There is no greater love relationship that you'll ever experience.

After I concluded the consecration, I went back to my old routine. I noticed the difference. Something was missing. I didn't have the calm serenity I experienced during that time. I missed my time with God. I missed talking to Him. I missed crying on His shoulder. I missed having Him soothe my spirit and soul. I missed Him. Those few months that I went without that fellowship, Jesus was wooing me with the incredible emptiness I felt. I knew I had to get back to that peace, joy and the release of basking in His presence. It returned immediately when I resumed our weekly meetings. What I found was incredible — He missed me too!

Engagement Ring

Do you have a place and time set aside just for you and Jesus? If so, use this time to not only pour out your requests to Him, but to also drink in the richness of His presence. If not, choose a place and time TODAY for a consistent rendezvous with your Savior.

Chapter 12

LIVING IN THE MOMENT

> **Ringmaster**
>
> *To every thing there is a season, and a time to every purpose under the heaven: A time to be born, and a time to die; a time to plant, and a time to pluck up that which is planted. Ecclesiastes 3:1-2*

Becoming engaged and active in your life requires work. A lot of work. In the initial stages of my journey, I thought it would be all fun and games. I was ready to experience all of the wonders of my life. I knew God had great things planned for me, and I couldn't wait to unwrap His magnificent gifts. What I slowly began to realize was that unfolding His plan took effort. It was quite surprising because I had been taught that whatever God had for you, He would put in close enough proximity that it wouldn't require great effort. I believed that if I had to work too hard to receive or obtain it, it wasn't God's will for me. As I began to study and reflect on His Word, I clearly saw that none of our forefathers had an easy path to greatness. No one traveling on his or her road of destiny is untouched by the "W" word — work.

Joseph is a clear example of this. Joseph, the dreamer, clearly saw his role as a leader as God began to deal with him through visions early in life. While in the midst of dreaming, I'm sure Joseph never envisioned being thrown - by his loving brothers nonetheless - in a cold, dank pit, being sold into slavery, then lied on by his boss' wife. I'm also certain the vision did not include his extended visit to jail and being forgotten and forsaken by the baker and cupbearer. This was Joseph's road to destiny and to his final destination as second in command in one of the greatest nations of the time. Yes, it had numerous speed bumps and a few potholes, but it was all a part of God's plan.

It takes enormous mental and physical stamina to fulfill your purpose and live in the present. It takes work to drink in all life is offering at any given moment. It is no easy task. Daily, I have to learn how to activate the five physical senses God graced us with. I'm still developing them as I seek to see the glory of each day, smell the beauty of the season, touch the petals of life, taste the plethora of flavors, and hear the sound of life teeming all around me. Sometimes it seems like a big job because I become so entrenched and focused on trivial distractions that I forget to be thankful for everything and every gift God gives.

I sometimes forget to thank Him for the gift of life, for good health, a great family, and close friends. I get so busy that it slips my mind to praise Him for shelter, clothing, daily food provision, a great job, a wonderful place to worship, good leadership, excellent parents and loving siblings. I'm running so hard and fast that I sometimes forget to celebrate the fact that I can see, I can walk, I can talk, I can hear, I can smell, taste, digest my food, dress and clothe myself, have presence of mind, can think clearly, can spell my name and know who I am and whose I am. We are so very blessed and highly favored of God to be alive.

Engagement Ring

Treat yourself to a walk in the park or a day in your back yard. Remove your shoes and feel the crisp blades of grass between your toes and the tiny grains of sand as they graze the bottom of your feet. Gaze into the sky – whether it is blue with white, puffy clouds or steel gray. Relish the knowledge that just for that day your heavenly Father ordered it just so. Inhale the scent of being in God's world – a world He created just for you!

Chapter 13

THE BEAUTY OF NOW

> **Ringmaster**
>
> *But by the grace of God I am what I am: and his grace which was bestowed upon me was not in vain; but I laboured more abundantly than they all: yet not I, but the grace of God which was with me. 1 Corinthians 15:10*

I have lived most of my life not really "in" my life. Oh, I was physically there, but I wasn't emotionally, spiritually or psychologically there. I used to be so focused at either living in my past or focusing on my future that I hardly ever enjoyed my day-to-day existence. Oh, if you saw me, I had a smile and pleasant demeanor for everyone. I was a joy to be around. But somewhere in the core of my being I lacked the true joy of living in the moment. I lived each moment waiting for a "better" moment.

I often move so swiftly toward the next goal in life that I scarcely take time to enjoy the moment or what I've come to acknowledge as the beauty of now. Each moment has its unique fingerprint. It is distinctive, priceless, and should never be taken for granted. Like a beautiful sunset slowly easing its way beyond the horizon, God blesses us with the beauty of a moment that will never repeat itself. You may see thousands of sunsets in a lifetime, but each will have its own distinction. That is the beauty of a now-moment. Not simply that we're here in the moment, but we experience something unique and precious. Our God is so creative that He didn't want a second to go by without showing us something beautifully new. It's as if He says, "If you thought that moment was special, take a look at this one."

Oh, for the peace to savor each moment in life and fully squeeze out every ounce of joy and excitement while in that one particular moment. Each moment is a time you will never see again. Although you can revisit it in your mind, you can never relive it in your life. It should be our goal to live every moment fully because we're not promised another one.

I am three people. Let me explain. One, I am a very strategic person; a planner. I like to map out my future in my mind. Whether it is career goals, family status or where I am going to eat dinner, I want to know in advance. I am the type of person who excels at mapping out five-year plans. I see something I want and immediately my mind goes to work devising a plan for the best, quickest and most sure way to get what it is I desire.

Second, I am also a dreamer. I can sit for hours dreaming the most elaborate plots and scenarios. I even had the impetus and groundwork for this book years before I actually sat down to pen it. The downside to being a dreamer is that you eventually have to come down to earth and actually put works to your vision.

Third, I am an analyzer. I can pick just about anything or any situation apart. It is a part of my drive or need for perfection, especially in myself. So if I wasn't planning or dreaming about a glorious future or my next wonderful project, I was dissecting my past and trying to understand what happened when something didn't go my way. I could spend months and I am embarrassed to admit years reliving something in my mind so I could understand my thought process during that time and revamp it so the same situations would not recur.

Reflection and introspection is good, but all of my rehearsing the past and planning the future was causing me to not enjoy the present. I couldn't bask in the beauty of the moment because I was always anticipating the next scene, event or occurrence. After years of this tennis match you can imagine that a sister was just plain tired. I was tired of rehearsing events I could not change and I was tired of dreaming about a future I did not have the courage to pursue. That is exactly what I was missing — courage.

It takes courage to live life fully. It takes presence of mind and a willingness to fail, be wrong and look silly to live totally in the moment. Living in the present meant that I would have to bring all of myself — my emotions, my mind and my body — into the here and now. It was a scary thought because if I did that I wouldn't have a safety net to catch myself if I fell or failed.

What I realized was the wall I had erected to keep failure and pain out was also shielding me from the glorious life God planned for me. It was a hard decision, but I came to the conclusion that I would rather experience the pain of hurt and disappointment if I failed than to live with the taunting of regret. You see, I learned you aren't really living if you know all of the answers. You are merely an actor in a scripted play. Not fully activating or participating in my life wasn't keeping life from moving on. Life was moving on without me. So I decided to throw caution to the wind, give God total control and free fall into the life He designed with me in mind. And yes, it is a wonderful life!

Engagement Ring

What dream have you shelved because you lacked the courage to pursue it? Look at it. Pray over it. Could this be your wake up call to dust off that dream and run with it? Write here what would happen if you pursued it? What would happen if you didn't?

Chapter 14

BE ALIVE

> **Rule of Engagement**
>
> Breathe in the beauty of each new day. Enjoy the innocent laughter of a child; bathe in the wisdom of your elders. Take the day off from being an adult. Shake off the inhibitions adulthood inevitably brings. Today you are simply God's child. Enjoy it!

Have you ever gazed into the playground and seen children laughing, smiling without a care and longed for that place of utter simplicity? I can remember when I was young how life was so easy. I came home to a warm house with two loving parents and three sometimes loving, but more so annoying big sisters. We always had a hot meal and warm bed to sleep in.

I never worried about who was paying the mortgage, electric bill and so forth. It never crossed my mind to be concerned about from where my next meal would come. I just trusted my earthly parents to provide everything I needed. That offered the incredible freedom for my siblings and me to just live. We could play without a care because we knew our parents loved us and would do anything necessary to care for us.

Well, I'm an adult now. This life as a grown up hasn't been what I expected nor anticipated. No one is paying my mortgage, car note or filling my pantry with groceries, but me. The carefree life I had enjoyed as a child was now riddled with so many responsibilities. That word — responsibilities — has encumbered many so-called adults. We get so bogged down with our day-to-day responsibilities we forget we have a heavenly Father anxiously waiting for us to look to Him.

I'm amazed at how many born-again Christians are not taking full advantage of Christ's sacrifice on the cross. We are so engrossed trying to make ends meet and survive that we've relinquished our position as children of God and have assumed the role of parent and creators of our destiny. We've laid down the great life Christ came to give us and have picked up the burden-laden existence of the enemy.

I learned one of the most valuable lessons ever in my visit to Nairobi, Kenya. It was perhaps the most life-changing event I had ever encountered. I simply was not prepared for the many mixed feelings I experienced. I was numb, excited, saddened and embarrassed all at the same time. I was numb because I saw myself everywhere. In the face of a young mother caring for her children, in the face of the college student scurrying to school, in the weathered face of an elderly woman in the bush country and in the face of the innocent school children. I was excited because I was getting the opportunity to see my history firsthand. I was their daughter, sister and friend. I felt so related to them, yet still a stranger.

And yes, I was saddened because I had never in all of my life witnessed such depravity. I could not believe anyone could be allowed to live in such deplorable situations. From the slums we visited, with no running water or electricity, to the schools that were exploding with more children than some small colleges, I was troubled. Who was going to help them? How could we fill such a great need? But into my chaotic musing came the giggling of a group of young children. Their bright eyes, curiously familiar faces and infectious grins embarrassed me. Here I was feeling sorry for them and they were the happiest children I'd ever seen. They were happy. They were content. No, they were thankful. They were thankful for a bottle of water, thankful for a smile from a stranger and thankful for a hug from their sister from across the water.

Though they had very little, nothing compared to most people, they knew what most of us struggle to comprehend. True happiness cannot be found in the latest model car, in mansions on a hill or in the fragile trappings we call success. They knew the value of family connections, true friendship and of being thankful for each day of life. I had never seen a more pure celebration of life as I watched them worship with reckless abandon as they thanked God for another day. I learned a valuable lesson from my brothers and sisters in Africa. It is the gift of thankfulness — for each day, for each moment and for each breath. I learned to view everyday as it is — a gift from God.

I believe it is a tragedy and affront to our Savior when we fail to be grateful and thankful for the awesome gift of life. How can we as Christians have the giver of life and refuse to live? To have life and then not live to me is almost a sin. We cannot let His sacrifice be in vain. We must make every effort to daily celebrate this wonderful gift of life until our clamorous celebration is so contagious that the entire planet wants in on the tremendous honor, blessing and privilege of being called His!

The Word says in John 10:10b, *"I am come that they might have life, and that they might have it more abundantly"* (KJV). We are privileged to have the giver of life living on the inside of us, and we must learn how to live. We must let go of our idea of what life is and grab hold to what His Word tells us about life. We must embrace the Word that says in Psalm 16:11, *"Thou wilt shew me the path of life: in thy presence is fulness of joy; at thy right hand there are pleasures for evermore."* His life and presence should bring us joy and that joy should filter out into all corners of the world. We should seek to be full of the light and life of Jesus. The world should be so captivated by the joy of the Lord they see emanating from us that they develop a burning desire to have Him too. Jesus stated in John 14:6, *"I am the way, the truth, and the life."* He is the only one who can really show us what it means to possess life and live the God-kind of life. The Word further states in I Peter 2:9, *"But ye are a chosen generation, a royal priesthood, an holy nation, a peculiar people; that ye should shew forth the praises of him who hath called you out of darkness into his marvellous light."* You were chosen and hand picked by God to live life in the glow of His light. As we leave the dismal darkness of a dreary, uninvolved life and draw closer to His light, we will see what it means to truly live in Him and for Him.

It has been a long journey and I am only beginning to learn how to become engaged in my life and truly live it. Every day I am better. I am learning to listen and love more and argue and complain less. I am less stressed and bothered by trivial things because I realize that they are light afflictions. I now know that everyone has struggles; we all have our burdens to bear. But the more I lean on my burden-bearer and release every issue to Him as soon as possible, the more peace I have in my life. I am the one in charge of the peace in my life. I can accept the weight of each issue or choose to release all anxiety by handing my problems to Jesus who is more than capable of handling them all.

I am now alive and vibrant. I love myself — exactly like God created me. I am His gift to my corner of the world. I enjoy and anticipate the beauty that each new day brings. I am excited about what God is doing in me and in those around me. I invite you into this celebration of life. You are beautiful and life is rich. Your life is God's gift to you and Him. Live it well.

ABOUT THE AUTHOR

Cheryl Thomas began her life of engagement June 12, 1968 in Gainesville, Florida. She is a daughter, sister, aunt, friend and licensed minister at *The Potter's House* in Dallas, Texas under the leadership of *Bishop T. D. Jakes*. The youngest of four daughters, this precocious youngster was always at the forefront of life — grabbing it by the horns.

But somehow the trials of life have a way of chipping away at the courage necessary to fully activate and participate in our own lives. We fall asleep at the wheel and become mere spectators in our own lives. Cheryl awoke from this state of lethargy in 2003 and since has made it her lifetime mission to fully "engage" in her life and squeeze the most out of the God-given gift of life. Her motto is Carpe Diem — Seize the day!

**Visit
Cheryl Thomas' website at:
www.BecomingEngaged.com
or
www.myspace.com/beengaged**

BECOMING ENGAGED™ ORDER FORM

Use this convenient order form to order additional copies of *Becoming Engaged*™

Please Print

Name_____
Address _____
City_____
State _____ ZIP _____
Phone _____
Email _____

_____ Copies of book @ ____ each $ _____

Postage and handling @ $____ per book $ _____

Total Amount Enclosed $ _____

Make Checks Payable to: *Becoming Engaged Enterprises*
Send to: *Becoming Engaged*™
P.O. Box 382764 • Duncanville, Texas 75138

www.ingramcontent.com/pod-product-compliance
Lightning Source LLC
LaVergne TN
LVHW041634070426
835507LV00008B/613